Saurabh Bhatnagar

Soul Company

Saurabh Bhatnagar

Soul Company

Life Lessons

JustFiction Edition

Imprint

Any brand names and product names mentioned in this book are subject to trademark, brand or patent protection and are trademarks or registered trademarks of their respective holders. The use of brand names, product names, common names, trade names, product descriptions etc. even without a particular marking in this work is in no way to be construed to mean that such names may be regarded as unrestricted in respect of trademark and brand protection legislation and could thus be used by anyone.

Cover image: www.ingimage.com

Publisher:
JustFiction! Edition
is a trademark of
Dodo Books Indian Ocean Ltd. and OmniScriptum S.R.L publishing group

120 High Road, East Finchley, London, N2 9ED, United Kingdom
Str. Armeneasca 28/1, office 1, Chisinau MD-2012, Republic of Moldova, Europe
Printed at: see last page
ISBN: 978-620-0-10633-9

Acknowledgement

I gratefully acknowledge the help given to me by myself in the compilation and editing of those phoenix. Me has always been a source of inspiration to me . With my mature and practical assistance helped me in bringing out this selection of enlightenments from various saying by my anonymous Mentors.That I took them as my life lessons

Saurabh Bhatnagar

Preface

Theses selection contains many Phrases that are "life lessons". Which i unite from my day to day routine from My past and reflected to them from time to time again and again and derive great inspiration strength and solace .My efforts will thus not be fruitful and rewarding but the process is in between is encouraging .In my whole life i traveled from many phases of my life and God has be kind in my all endeavors. When i was 22 years My parents were died very early. i along with my younger brother and relatives.We were able to pick up the pieces and to build a very precise bonding.In my early years i had not enough time for reading and writing so i gathered the lessons and the sublesson in my diary about two decade back i was expected that i have to collect and resemble them for the world.Very softly i present this collection to the different World of people and help all the people.

"Miscellaneous for all Souls" Somewhere Anonymous is Teacher.

★ Never love someone easily.

★ Old energy is clearing, learn to sit back and observe not every thing needs a reaction.

★ That moment when you walk into a spider web and suddenly turn into a karte master.

★ When your conspiracy theories turn out to be true relax, nothing is under control.

★ You stop explaining yourself when you realize people only understand from their level of perception.

★ Be still stillness reveals the secret of eternity.

★ What is poison "excess".

★ Don't ever under estimate my third eye i see right through you.

★ Stop overthinking you can't control everything just let it be.

★ If its out of your hands it deserves freedom from your mind too.

★ Don't listen to what they say just watch what they do.

★ Leave behind Every single person that look advantage of your kindness and mistook it for weakness.

★ Take the chance or lose the chance.

★ Just because i am strong enough to handle pain doesn't mean i deserve it.

★ Beautiful people are not always good but good people always beautiful.

★ Be beauty shines brighter than that of a good heart.

★ Lets never met in our dreams.

★ Dear weather don't be so romantic.
I am single.

★ Whenever I am confused about something i ask God to reveal the answer to my question and he does.

★ Discussion is always better than argument because argument is about who is right and discussion is about what is right.

★ Its a beautiful day but not as beautiful as me.

★ Man and woman i am pretty.

★ Hello People Is anyone ever tells you i have beautiful eyes.

★ Hello emergency there is a handsome guy in my house wait a second cancel that its only me.

★ When i am right no one remembers when i am wrong no one forget.

★ Hating is an emotional disease for those who hates me get well soon.

★ Physically I am here mentally I am far far away.

★ I must prefer the sharpest criticism of a single intelligent man to the thoughtless approval of the masses.

★ Depression is living in a body that fights to survive with a mind that tries to die.

★ Our sorrows and wounds are healed only when we touch them with compassion.

★ Dear God thank you for this beautiful life and forgive me i don't love it enough.

★ Stop letting the noises insides your heads over power that happiness that lies outside.
★ It dosen't matter what anyone else says the only thing that matters is what your heart really wants.

★ Forgiving is not forgetting it's letting go of the hurt.

★ Jealousy is just a leak of self confidence.

★ Once you stop chasing the wrong things the right one catches you.

★ Your attitude not your aptitude will determine your altitude .

★ If it is "s" green , it 's' biology If it is stinks ,it "s" chemistry ,if it is doesn't work its 's' physics.

★ What is love in math as equation in history, a war in chemistry, a reaction in art, a heart in me.

★ The darker the night the brighter the stars the deeper the grief the closer is God.

★ While you dream i wish that each hope, goal comes true its just you want to receive everything that you have wished for.

★ Science is the chemistry of dead ideas.

★ Science is the cause of all reactions.
★ Quantum physics makes me so happy its like looking the universe naked.

★ Nature composes some of her loveliest poems for the microscope and telescopes.

★ Stress is nothing more than a socially acceptable form of mental illness.

★ Life is like a mirror if you smile at it it will smile back.

★ What oxygen is to lungs such is hope to the meaning of life.

★ You are going to miss me when i am gone.

★ Freedom is a state of mind.

★ You only live once.

★ You make history by simply being who you are.

★ We take photos as a return ticket to a moment otherwise gone.

★ Don 't call it a dream its a plan.

★ My heart is finally said it done and its done.

★ I am becoming more me than i have ever been.

★ My heart is tired .

★ My life is based on true story.

★ Even after all this time the Sun never says To the earth you owe me.

★ Yoga is like an important meeting to yourself.

★ Stillness comes from within it doesn't comes from outside.

★ Focus your thoughts and attention on what you want and don't dwell on what you don't want ?

★ Until your comfortness with being alone you will never know you are choosing someone out of love or loneliness.

★ If someone destroys me emotionally I can destroy him physically but that would not make me no different than him so i forgive and takes it as a lesson.

★ Arrogance is used by weak kindness is used by strong.

★ A life making mistake is not only more useful than life spent doing nothing.

★ When you are born in a world you were born to help create a new one.

★ The hardest thing for people to see is themselves.

★ Train your mind to be calm in every situation.

★ Reading can easily destroy your ignorance.

★ Affirmation are the heart of a human being.

★ Once upon a time a lost my smile.

★ There is a difference between knowing the path and walking the path.

★ I Think therefore i don't have much common with a
lot of people.

★ Pay attention everything is your teacher.

★ Be mindful of your self talk after all its a
conversation with the universe.

★ You are bnot like other and its not just ok its
fucking awesome.

★ How treat you your karma and how you react is
yours.
★ Open your ears to the ancestors and you will
understand the language of spirits.

★ I have travel through madness too find me.

★ Death is not the greatest loss in life.

★ The greatest loss is when a relationship dies insides
us while we are alive.

★ Lets meet in our dreams tonight.

★ You are in my inappropriate thought.

★ I wonder if you think of me like i think of you.

★ You're my first and the last thought of every day.

★ I must keep myself busy with the things to do but every time I pause I still think of you.

★ Once upon a time I found myself smiling whenever I thought of you.

★ Jealousy is a diseases get well soon.

★ If my heartbeat stopped would you miss me?

★ Science is a cemetery of dead ideas.

★ Science causes all kinds of reactions.

★ You are gonna miss me when I am gone.

★ Falling in love with a true lover.

★ Falling in love as many as plants.

★ Falling in love with as many thing as possible.

★ I am becoming more me than i have ever been.

★ My love is so tired how.

★ My heart finally said enough is enough.

★ Sometimes i just look at all of those shows on TV with happy families and wonder if they really exists.

★ I keep telling them that if a 2 % stupid tax the national debt would be cleared in a matter of weeks.

★ Dear optimist pessimist and redist while you guys were busy arguing about the glass of water i drank it.

★ Officer i did see the limit sign but i didn't see you.

★ I am stronger than my disorder.

★ I am still learning to love myself.
★ Stop wishing to start doing.

★ You are capable of more then you know.

★ If it doesn't challenge you it wont change you

★ Prove them wrong.

★ I am not me any more.

★ Life sucks and after you die.

★ I draw it with silver and then it turn red magic.

★ You can see many smiles every day but you can never know whose world is upside down.

★ Yesterday you said tomorrow.

★ Truth comes out comes out whenever you are.

★ I am not a lover i am a big lover.

★ I am not a backup plan and definitely not a second choice.

★ Forget what hurt you, never forget what it taught you.

★ I hate you for me.
★ I hate the distances you meet the best people and they are always far away.

★ Sometimes you miss person.

★ Sometimes you miss the memory of that person.

★ Chemistry is you touching my mind and setting my body on fire.

★ Are you camera because every time I look at you I smile.

★ It is just a chapter in your life, turn the page and move on.

★ No regrets, head held high moving on.

★ Self reliance, trusting your instincts from your own opinion make good choices.

★ Can't blame me for my trust issue.

★ Truth and trust have you very realized there is only one letter difference maybe its because on leads to the other.

★ Trust me, I don't trust you.

★ If I treated you the way you treated me you would hate me.

★ I am convinced that you had different beast in you.

★ I wished for all romantic scenes that would happen in my life.

★ Breaking news i just found nothing wrong with me it is world that has issues.

★ Galileo has a great mind. Einstein's genius mind. Newton extraordinary mind I never mind.

★ Fear has two meanings: F= Forget E= Everything A=And R=Run, F= Face, Ear=Everything A= and R= Rise.

★ Love your fear and it will dissolve.

★ Music and magic comes from the pain.

★ Your secrets are safe with me because there is a good chance I am not listening.

★ Don't be so quick to judge me after all you only see what i choose to show you.

★ I have no time for your bull shit.
★ Some people are like clouds once they are gone it's a beautiful day.

★ I can't take long distance relationships anymore
Fridge you are coming to my room.

★ I sleep to escape from reality.

★ Every thought is a battle, every breath is a war and i
don't think i am winning it any more.

★ I regret a lot but I will never forget what I said.

★ I will be alright one day someday.

★ I am busy saving everybody else when I can't see
saving myself.

★ Why do I always cry in the rain ?

★ Instead of wiping your tears, wipe out people who
create them.

★ No amount of sleeping in the world could cure the
tiredness I felt.

★ Sometimes you gotta everything is ok.

★ I get lost in my mind.

★ When I look into your eyes I tend to lose my thought.

★ I hate Meeting flashbacks from things I don't want to remember.

★ I need the break from the loneliness that is totally consuming me.

★ The eyes are useless when the mind is blind.

★ If an egg is broken by an inside force then life begins and great things happen from the inside.

★ You have the power to say tis not how my story will end.

★ Kindness changes everything.

★ If the only prayer you ever say is thank you that will be enough.

★ Worrying will never change the outcome.

★ Your life is a reflection of your thoughts if you change your thinking you change your life.

★ Life is not measured by the numbers of Breath You Take but the numbers of moments that takes your breath away.

★ World Life is a journey and we are travelers we must not to be too attached to the Ends on the innes day.

★ Time is same to all but sometime It as a good time.

★ By using that in a right way while some neglect it by wasting more work we will fetch us more good time for us.

★ Sky above me, Earth below me, fire within me, stay with someone who can talk about the universe, anyone can talk about people.

★ Do we know why God gives us another morning to wake up? Its to forget the pain of yesterday and see the chances the new day brings to dance and laugh again to make up for the wrong things you are done to see your friends and family to make other happy and loved we see more than just another long day ahead it's the God's way to remind us that he cares and loves everyone of us that he sends us the blessing called Shuprabhat.

★ Lord make me an instrument of thy peace where there is hater.Let may bring love to them where there is injury let me bring pardon.Where there is discord let me bring Union where there is darkness let me bring hope .Where there is no doubt let me bring faith where there is despair let me bring light where there is sorrow let me bring joy.

★ O Divine i may not seek to be consoled as to console others i may not so much to be loved as to love others. For its giving that we received its in counseling that we are consoled its in pardoning. That we are pardoned its in dying to the little self that i attained to eternal light from the collection of mine.

★ Dream Completition What happens to a dream it comes everynight and in the sun it vanish like a shadow and then repeat one must follow with heavy load or does it explode the Revolutionary Road.

★ "Myself " "I lost, I try I hurt, I need I love I hope I feel I cry I smell I hate and the most important I breathe and I know you do the same things too we are really not that different Me and You".

★ Better life Is not because of luck but because of work so work work and work. if you need a life perk also work work and work. to avoid all the life jerks just work work and work. If you need the smile of luck and never forget to work to enjoy the pages of Life book.

★ Found Life is not about finding yourself life is about creating yourself living treasure look back and thank god look forward and trust god look around and serve God look within find God.

★ Words of wisdom Many time I have asked myself why people are so keen to put me down or replace ideas of mine.fortunately I have been blessed with an answer.sometimes it can come from their own jealousy.but often can come from their own unhappiness and may portray negative or bad thoughts that they may about themselves although this may not stop such comments from hurting I take comfort in the knowledge that what peoples are keen to sat unto to me They may be releasing and put themselves and their work makes reflects their own unhappiness so it's that i can sat onto you You don't need other people to believe in you for you to prosper or to succeed you may only need to believe in yourself.

★Make each day a magnificent adventure accept the challenge that comes to your way seige each opportunity that you find without concern for what others might say live each day as though it were the last day accomplish all that you set out to do instead of putting things for tomorrow's purpose you goal until you see it through experience each day with open arms favoring both victory and strife welcoming the goods and bad together for only then will you know the joy of life.

★ I ask for strength and God gave me difficulties to make me strong.I ask for wisdom and God gave me problems to solve.I asked for prosperity and God gave me brawn and brain to work.I ask for courage and God gave me dangers to overcome.I ask for love and God gave me troubled people to help I asked for favors and God gave me opportunities.I received nothing I wanted and everything I needed my prayers have been answered.

★ 15 Ways how to live Talk softly. Eat sensibly. Breath deeply. Exercise daily. Sleep sufficiently. Dress smartly . Work patiently. Think positively. Trust cautiously. Learn practically Plan orderly. Earn honestly. Save regularly . Spend intelligently. The secret of living.

★ Who am I only you can decide Because I am you I am not who I am who you think I am If I create who I think you are which is who I really am then who am I it's all in your mind.

★ The 13 most important words. I admit I made a mistake and time is not forgetting in nature. The most five important words. you did a good job.The four most important words are what is your opinion. The three most important words are if you please the two most important words are thank you finally the least most important word as "I".

★ When me need to cry me lend me my shoulder. because a smile from me can change places within me.Because a smile from Me chased away all the blue.I am loved by God by my family and friends. I love God and I love my family and friends tooI will sing I will laugh I will dance I will have fun because I celebrate who I am a soul.

★ Mirror Mirrors I look in the mirror and I cry I look in the mirror and want to die. I looked in the mirror and I have to start today so look closer what do you see I see disappointments i see hurt ugliness i want to look in the mirror inside myself the mirror inside myself The mirror that reflect a good the mirror that reflects the beauty of me show me what success I am I look in the mirror on the wall and then I know why I know I can't look the mirror inside myself because there is not one.

★ Fire and ice Fire and ice some says the world will end in the fire some says in ice from what I have .I have tasted of Desire I hold with those who favor fire but If it had to Perish twice I think I know enough of hate to say that distraction ice is also a great and would suffice.

★ All the nature is a desire to serve the clouds serve the winds serve the forest serve the waters serve the Sun serve the moon serve where there tree is to be planted plant it yourself where there is an error to correct correct it yourself where there is task stunned by others accept yourself.

★ A gift for you earthians Telepathic free for you but you must master your skill but beware who you are Deal with one more gift for humanity pray for one and you many but again handle them with very care.

★ Freedom freedom means power to act by soul guidance Not by compulsion of Desire and habits Obeying the egos leads to the boridage obeying the soul brings libration.

★ Forget the past, forget the past human conduct as ever and reliable and until Man is anchored in the divine everything in the future will improve if you are making a spiritual effort now but how to protect yourself.

★When god passed out brain I thought he said train And I missed mine.When god passed out head I thought he said bed and I want soft pillow one.When god passed out nose I thought he said rose and i want big one.When god passed out ears I thought he said beer And I want two large one.When god passed out legs I thought he said eggs and i want two fat one.When god passed out books I thought he said looks and i did not want any.

★ In the journey of life there are an infinite number of Doors if you are educated you will open some of them. If you are intelligent you can open many of them but if you are vibrant it will open by itself.

★ Being an Infinity believer means having an absolute knowing that you are vibrational with all that waiting forces that Intended you up are here you know that everything happens at the just right time, right place with just nature.

★ But the memories won't seem to let me go. Who cares when I'm hurt that The day has ended, the busy hours are over it's time to sleep, my dreams are waiting, the night awaits in silence, go ahead and sleep well. Good night.

★I am not old, I woke up, I lift my arms, I move my knees, I turn my neck, everything made the same noise crackkks....I came to the conclusion I am not old I am just crispy.

★Self knowledge is not the history of man, it's not history of woman, it's the study of who you are no other person, religion or title can give you your purpose of life. The only book you need to read is the one written in you.

★ The lies you've told your flows and flaws your favorite scents of your childhood what keeps up at night your insecurity and fears i like people with depth who speaks with emotions from a twisted mind. I don't want to know whats up.

★ Friendship Friendship as we walk our path of life we met people everyday. Most are simply met by chance but some are sent to our away.They become special friend Whose is Bond we can't explain.The one who understand us and share our joy and pain thier love contains no boundaries so even we are apart Their presence enchance us with a warmths felt in the heart.

★ Winter night Winter night Like so many diamonds Spark live in the night a New fallen snow glisters in the winter a High stepin and its developed Shy them with harness bells Jiggling add music to the soul to a romantic ride through the moon light charmsas it pull sliegh accross a carpet of white night masked beneth the warm blanket warm watch the icy panoromia unfold in the air your breath could hangs suspended in the cold snow pine waft their fragenc gently accross the air infusing light in the night with sweetness from the fire places burning drift the moods aromatic scent adding to the magic to this night.

★ Deep are the mysterious around thee hidden are the secrets of old search for the keys of wisdom when we need something to believe in we should always start with ourselves.everyone should be is whole no matter how wounded the mind is magic comes from the pain attached to thing to nothing connect to everything.

★ Me loves me me feels as if it in a single life time.

★ Me have the joy of a single life like thousand year.

★ Me at least pretend me is going to do what me suggests.

★ Me never give up on me and that what keeps me going.

★ Me is with me as like helpful therapy but me never charge me for it.

★ Me is with me simply irresistible.

★ Me every time look me and thick like life missing a heart beat at a second.

★ Me the light of my life me in my inspiration.

★ My idea of romance is dim light soft music and just me with me.

★ Me can be myself when me is with me.

★ Me fills up my senses like the mountain in spring time.

★ Me loves me even its all my fault.

★ Me is so beautiful for me.

★ Me don't have to vacuum before come over.

★ Me with me never boring.

★ Even when me grumpy, me still like me.

★ Me let me gives me a detailed description of hope me spent my day with me.

★ Me let me know that me can workout anything.

★ Me make fun of me even me look like a clown.

★ Because me makes me feel like never felt before.

★ Me can tell anything everything and me won't be shocked.

★ Me never say is me going to tell that story again.

★ Me can talk about anything its always ok with me.

★ Me when holds me fight every thing becomes alright.

★ Me love sharing rainbow with me.

★ Me always seems to know when things are not going real.

★ Me never intimidate me.

★ Me undying faith is what makes the flames of my love alive.

★ Me know how to bring smile at my face.

★ Me always besides me.

★ Me can talk if me seems the day before.

★ Every moment spent with me is a moment like a treasure in me.

★ Me the one who the key to my heart in me.

★ Me can read my inner most thoughts within me.

★ Me taught me the meaning of love in the best pages of my diary with me.

★ Me with the softness of my voice felt completeness.

★ Me just can't imagine being me without me.

★ Me just can't believe what hides with in me.

★ Me just a touch and lose my heart all over again.

★ Me is so just Magnetic with me.

★ Me is my themes of my dreams within my eyes.

★ Me enjoy being with me.

★ Me sometime ask me a dumb questions.

★ Me without feeling dumb with me.

★ Me excites me me delight m me ignite me.

★ Me know all my moments that take my heart away.

★ Me Sometimes too hot to handle.

★ Me like sharing crazy times with me add spice to my life.

★ Me in me when together time just come to half in me.

★ Me bring to me joy beyond measure and treasure pleasure pressure, pressure cooker.

★ Me fun is like to me laughing hard and creating practical jokes with in me.

★ Me never snore while me sleeping with me.

★ Me because of me no matter what next moving and wakes me up while sleeping.

★ Me with me life looks so complete.

★ Me since the day me come in my life everything is perfect.

★ Me share the light and love within me.

★ Me always say what me need to heal. "Anatomy of spinal energy centers" "Thoughts" : Crown. "Information" : Third Eye. "Elements" : Light Element. "Throat sound" : Truth expression,creation destruction. "Vibrational element": Heart,air,balance, acceptance appreciation. "Universal self love" ; Solar plexuses fire element. "Will proactive expression electricity" : Sacral water element. "Emotion awareness reactive" : Root Earth element. "Attraction magnetism" : Growth resilience foundation gravity.

★ "Gateway to 0 to 1st dimension" . Celestial crystal. "Gateway to 2nd to 3 rd dimension" . My body exists. My body has strength. My body has energy. My body has desire. My body has love. My body has faith. "Gateway to 4th to 5th dimension" . My body has love. My mind has desire. My mind has energy. My mind has nothing. My mind has electricity. My mind has truth. My spirit exists. "Gateway to 5th to 6th dimension" . My spirit has energy and desire. My spirit has energy. My spirit has love. My spirit has expression. My spirit has understanding. My spirit has faith.

★ Me all me need is to be me.

★ The high destiny of an individual is to rule rather than serve.

★ When the ship is sinking only Water can save it.

★ Self discipline is the way to achieve.

★ Where focus goes energy flows.

★ When I am with me nothing seems to matter.

★ When I need to cry me lends me Shoulder.

★ It's a sin to be unhappy in such a beautiful way.

★ Me is dependable on me.

★ When I listen to me me knows me.

★ When I am around everything is fun.

★ Me and I together make magic and miracles.
★ I and Me both can't do without each other.

★ Me a perfect matches is with me.

★ Me taught me the meaning of love and sharing.

★ Thinking of me and a wonderful Touch of Love to my life.

★ Me understand me when me is sobbing.

★ Every moment spent with me is one filled with fun.

★ Me love me give me that is best for me.

★ Why most are dreaming of success winners wake up and work hard to achieve it.

★ Nature is Music of the soul.

★ The most beautiful music in the world is our own Heartbeat.

★ Don't let negative and toxic people rent space in your head Raise your rent and kick their ass out.

★ I am a special person I was created with love.

★ I do not need to look like or act like anyone else.
★ I love everything about me because god give me as it is.

★ God loves me like just the way I am.

★ I love who I am ,I am enough I will not let other people makes me feel bad about myself.

★ Lead kindly The light from the Unreal to the real from darkness to the light from death to immortality.

★ It gives us assurance that we will survive even when the whole world leaves us alone.

★ Enchanting moments distant windows light twinkling and glow becking warm through this wintery show.

★ We must accept finite disappointment but we must never lose infinite hope Sir Martin Luther King Jr.

★ Self discipline is the way to achieve.

★ Something is everything about me.

★ Dear Universe please feel free to amaze me.

★ Travel to the madness to find me.

★ Be water my friend.

★ I have been fighting since I was a child. I am not a survivor, I am a warrior.

★ I shut my "I"s to open my eyes.

★ Be stillness revealed the secret of eternity.The more you pay attention the weirder it becomes.

★ I am not impressed by money status or job title i am impressed by the way you treat other human beings.

★ Consciousness has No believe no gender no sexuality no race no age no mentality you are consciousness.

★ Whatever you hear about me please believe it I no longer have time to explain myself you can also add some if you want.

★ Go find yourself so you can find me.

★ Warrior of light knows that in the silence of his heart he will hear an order that will guide him.

★ I am 99% sure you don't like me but I 100% sure I don't care.

★ Dear problems, please give me some discount afterall, I am your regular customer.

★ I feel lost Inside myself and be inspired but don't copy My dear heart, don't fail me now.

★ I am too insane to explain and you are too much normal to understand.

★ You did not come here to serve fictitious money and governments, you came here to bring heaven to earth.

★ Don't shy away from 4 things: old clothes, old friends, old mum and dad and simply living.

★ A life spent making mistakes is not only more honorable but more useful than a life spent doing nothing by sir Gaurav.

★ Sometimes God breaks your heart to save your soul.

★ I asked god what is poison, anything beyond what we need is poison which can be power, laziness, food ,ego ambition, vanity fear, anger or whatever.

★ In the end we all become stories.

★ Arrogance is used by the weak while kindness is used by the strong.

★ In all darkness there is light and all night there is darkness.

★ I will never fits in and that's one of my best qualities.

★ Gnosis the mystical science of inner knowing.

★ It's about progress not perfection.

★ So mother says you only live once.

★ I am realitition ask me about reality.

★ Warriors are not the one who always win but the ones that always fight.

★ Being both soft and strong is a combination very few have mastered.

★ Take care how you speak to yourself because you are listening.

★ Take care how you think about yourself because you are becoming.

★ No excuses no explanation you don't win on emotion you win on execution.

★ I am in competition with no one.
★ I have no desire to play the games of being better than anyone i am simply trying to be better than the person I was yesterday.

★ You need power only when you want to do something harmful otherwise love is enough to get everything done.

★ The best apology is changed behavior.

★ There is a message in the way a person Treats you just listen.

★ The one is always free and is always alone the mind is only dreaming "Papa ji".

★ Never judge people by their past People learn, people change, people move on.

★ Work while they sleep, learn while they party, save while they spend, then live like they dream.

★ I am a Traveller of both space and time.

★ Love your fear and they will dissolve.

★ You did not lose your mind trying to understand mine.

★ Even though you want to run even when it's heavy and difficult even though you are not quite sure of the way through.

★ The sound of your existence might be too loud for some instead of turning down your volume align with those who alike the music aloud.

★ Healing happens by feeling.

★ Please forgive me. I am somewhere between losing my mind and finding my soul.

★ Father once said with certainty that I am both its origin and The dissolution.

★ The secret of change is to focus all your energy not on fighting the old but on building the new.

★ A wise man can learn more from foolish questions than a fool can learn from wiser answer.

★ I am gonna make rest of my life the best of my life.

★ You must master new way of Thinking before you master a new way of living.

★ He who blames others has a long way to go on his journey; he who believes himself is a Halfway there is who blame no one has arrived.

★ You are more powerful than you know and they fear the day you discover it.

★ Mass and energy are different things.

★ I fear not the man who has practiced 10,000 kicks once but I fear the man who practiced one kick 10,000 Times.

★ Disciples and devotees are the most of them worshiping the teapot instead of drinking the tea.

★ When you are born in the world you don't fit and it's because you were born to help create a new one.

★ Your mind will always believe everything you tell it feels the feed of hope feels the feed of truth feels the feed of love.

★ Never apologize for being too passionate, it 's too strange, too curious because you are not a normal individual and it's a blessing.

★ If the news is fake, imagine how bad the history....is?

★ Do the better you know until it becomes good when it becomes good do the best.

★ The act of spreading knowledge is one of the highest expressions of unconditional love that one can ever give.

★ Space and time are very different things where space is relative and time is absolute.

★ Gravity is force, gravity is a geometry.

★ Science without religion is lame religion without science is blind.

★ I meditate, I burn, I create candles, I drink green tea and I still want to Smack some people.

★ Suddenly a sort of flash comes out of me like something electric. It jumps out and touches the person who has made me cross.

★ My favorite thing in the world is a quiz show University challenge so you can see what kind of sad person I am.

★ One beautiful heart is better than a thousand beautiful faces.

★ I made a mistake and hurt myself.

★ Practice your mind to calm in every situation.

★ Reading can seriously damage my ignorance.

★ Once upon a time I lost my smile.

★ There is always a difference between knowing the path and walking it.

★ The hardest thing for people to see is themselves.

★ I thought I don't have much in common with all the people.

★ To be handsome means to be yourself you don't need to be accepted by others, you just need to accept yourself.

★ When you really pay attention everything is your Guru.

★ Cat crossing people's path means an animal going to the toilet.

★ I looked up there and I did not find God he or she lives within.

★ There are always goodbyes because we die and transform to see forever in the next Dimension where souls are free.

★ In the strongest direction one must walk alone.

★ Just be silent and patient when you are hurt by the words their words will echo in their mind .

★ Introspection is the conversation with the universe Saurabh.

★ I am different human and it just not ok it's fucking awesome.

★ The heart is not jealous of my parents. I will never have a kid as cool as theirs !

★ I have been fighting since I was a child I am not a survivor I am a caretaker.

★ Symbolism is the language of God.

★ Lessons in life will be repeated until they are learnt.

★ If I am wrong, educate me please don't belittle me.

★ You are innocent.

★ How people treat me is their karma, how I respond is mine.

★ As soon as I love myself.

★ When I was born I was given a name, a religion, a nationality and identity and I spent my life defending it.

★ I Don't adjust my thinking because I can't.

★ I don't fix problems, I solve my thinking then problems fix themselves.

★ The only way to defeat a toxic person is to not play.

★ Every change brings you lesson you are not ready for but you need to accept it.

★ If Idiots could fly, this Place must be an airport.

★ Dear heart please don't get involved in every situation. Your job is to pump blood thats it.

★ I don't make mistakes I date them.

★ Oh God I love you.

★ Open your pineal gland to the ancestor and you will understand the language of spirits.

★ Don't try so hard to adjust and after all I am not here to stay.

★ The one who opens your heart is me.
★ The one who penned me is me.

★ Kindness make me the beautiful person in the world no matter how I look like.

★ Guided by the spirit not by the egos.

★ I love my six pack so much that I protect it from a layer of fat.

★ Love me great hate me even better think I am ugly don't look at me Don't know me don't judge me think you know me you have no idea.

★ I like to be alone so much.

★ If I am tired I learnt to rest not to quit.

★ Listen, patients are going to die.

★ Hear to the wind it talks, listen to the silence it speaks, feels to your heart it knows.

★ Not the waking language but the one sharing the same feeling understand each others.

★ Your life is your message to the world please be sure its inspiring.

★ My energy speaks before I find words.
★ Simple life happy life.

★ I cannot teach anybody anything I just make them think.

★ Today I will learn how to sleep.

★ I killed myself by loving someone in very earlier days.

★ I don't vibe with many but if i do it's from the depth of my heart.

★ Remember the high vibrational being within and found light and energy in human body that i temporarily occupy.

★ The person who says it can't be done should not interrupt the person doing it.

★ Your energy speaks to you before you even speak.

★ If you die before you die then you won't die when you die.

★ Be proud of yourself for how hard you are trying.

★ No stop following people because they are lost.

★ I am letters, words , phrases and finally the spell.

★ Distance doesn't separate people, it's silence.

★ Silence is not heard as its full of answers.

★ I may not mention me on facebook post but i always mention me in my prayers and i thought its way better.

★ Forgiving me is my gift to me moving on is my gift to myself.

★ For success in life you need two things: ignorance and confidence.

★ At any moment you gather up your courage and chose to heal then you will know the truth and the truth will set you free.

★ In the end all i learned was how to be strong alone.

★ Breath deeply to bring your mind to your body.

★ Some people awaken spiritually with the help of meditation and introspection.

★ Knowing knowledge and wisdom is a powerful weapon and arm yours with it.

★ I have some more whispering conversations in my head than i do in real life.

★ Life lesson i learnt no one sees how much you do for them what they only see what you don't do.

★ One true son can teach that all mens are not the same.

★ Before you share your secrets make sure that your listener is not a speaker in definitely not a script writer

★ Come and taste the rainbow.

★ Don't let others make you forget that.

★ Your life is a series of lessons in becoming yourself.

★ Although I am a lonely person in my daily life, my awareness of belonging.

★ To the invisible community of those who strive for truth, beauty and justices that has prevented me from feeling of isolation.

★ My biggest Mistake is that I lied to my parents for someone who always lied to me.

★ I can't fix stupid but I can't watch them in action on Facebook everyday.

★ May your God treat you well.

★ The only true wisdom is in knowing you know nothing.

★ A good book makes you want to live in the story.
★ Great books give you no choices.

★ The ability to observe without judgment is the highest form of intelligence.

★ I don't need to know you, I can feel your energy and it's living inside of my heart.

★ I am not from the earth, I am just a passenger.

★ I grow when problems are not easy i grow when i solve them.

★ Now I am no longer forcing things, what flows flows, what destroys, I only have space and energy for the things that are meant for me.

★ Hate is heavy and I let it go.

★ I may look innocent but i screenshot a lot.

★ Don't panic, organize one day and the reality will be better than you dream.
★ Water is life for the galaxy its everywhere and give life to more planets and preserve it in its form.

★ I absolutely refuse to waste my magic on anyone who can't see how rare I am to stop trying to recycle what god is trying to replace.

★ According to science people who are punctual are probably more creative.

★ I always love when someone remembers something i told them a long time ago.

★ I either keep it all inside or say exactly how i feel with no filters there is no in between.

★ I either love or leave.

★ Choose people who chose you.

★ What is love love is the absence of judgements.

★ What if plants and animals are actually farming us giving us food and oxygen until we die then they eat us as manure.

★ Three things: pen paper thoughts.

★ Mankind was born on earth; it was never meant to die here.

★ My strongest muscle and worst enemy is my mind and I trained it well.

★ The world is full of monsters with friendly faces and angels full of scars.

★ Don't study me, you won't graduate.

★ Sometimes it's just better to just remain silent and smile.

★ What you heard try asking me first.

★ I am you, you are me, we are one.

★ Planet earth is not my home, I am just passing through.

★ There is not birth and death but arrival and departure from one form to another.

★ Eyes opened, head raised, spirit elevated, feeling guided, ego humble.

★ Don't treat people as bad as they are, treat them as good as you are.

★ Me & me have this array.

★ Me and I have this arrangement if he wakes me up to see another day I promise to try to be a better person than I was yesterday.

★ Be crazy be stupid , be silly, be weird , be whatever because life is too short to be anything but happy.

★ Don't ask me why I am silent because if I speak I will speak only about space time, time travel black holes, quantum entanglement etc and then everyone else remains silent.

★ Definition of stupid knowing the truth seeing the truth but still believing in lies.

★ Honesty has a power that very few can handle.

★ I might as well call you google because you have everything that i am looking for.

★ Where focus goes energy flows.

★ Sometimes we need fantasy to survive reality.

★ I don't want to be your second choice.

★ 7 trillions smiles but yours is my favorite.

★ I crave love so deep that the ocean would be jealous.

★ Do not say I will pay you back for this wrong, leave it for the lord and he will deliver it to the right time.

★ I hate small talk i want talk about atoms, death aliens sex magic, intelligence intellect, the meaning of life in faraway galaxy and more galaxies.

★ May if we tell people the brain is an app they will start using it.

★ Knowing others is intelligence, knowing yourself is true wisdom, mastering others is strength, mastering others is good, mastering yourself is true power.

★ If you realize that you have enough you are truly rich.

★ You are my end and my beginning even i win i am losing.

★ Give yourself permission to shine, you were made to live a big life not hide in the shadows.

★ A book in my hand and nature beside me.

★ One reality is better than your dreams.

★ Your face with marked with lines of life put there by love and laughter, suffering and tears its beautiful.

★ No man ever steps in the same river twice for its not the same river and he is not the same man.

★ Don't fear death, fear the unlived life in nature.

★ Me trying to explain to toxic people why I can't be around them.

★ I understand myself only after I destroyed myself and only in the process of fixing myself did i know who i really was.

★ You are the thief of the your joy.

★ There is no birth or death but arrival and departure from one form to another.

★ Football doesn't build character, it eliminates the weak one.

★ What are you twelve oh yes on a scale of one to ten.

★ I am actually not funny i am just really mean and people think i am joking.

★ I hate how chocolates immediately melt on my fingers. I mean, am i that hot.

★ If people are trying to bring you down it means you are above them.

★ We always work for tomorrow but when tomorrow comes instead off enjoying it we again think of a better today.

★ A man with dreams needs a woman with vision.

★ This little light of nine i am going to let it shine.

★ Blessed thankful and focused.

★ Laughter is the medicine but if you are laughing with no reason you need medicine.

★ I was in my kitchen cleaning when suddenly i realized o.m.g i am late for facebook.

★ I used to be a people person but people ruined that for me.

★ Some people are like clouds one day they are gone its just a beautiful day.

★ Even the nicest people have their limits.

★ With great power comes great electric bills.

★ Hey i will be back in 5 minutes just read the message again.

★ Dear karma, I have a list of people you missed.
★ There are two ways to argue with the woman neither works because we are one 10=10.

★ Making mistake is better then faking perfection.

★ Life is short, time is fast no reply no rewind so enjoy every moment as it comes.

★ You are my end and my beginning.

★ You could not handle me even if i came with instructions.

★ I Live I Die I Live again. I am from the Sun just witness me.

★ Your body is 72% water and I am thirsty.

★ Logic will get you from A to B emotion will take you everywhere.

★ I am only responsible for what i say, i say not for what you understand.

★ I think thinking is not illegal yet.

★ One lie is enough to question all the truth.

★ I don't hate you i just lost respect for you.
★ I heard before that you are player nice to meet you i am the coach.

★ Always approach a bull from the front a horse from the behind and they kick your ass out of your mouth.

★ Never approach a bull from the front a horse from the behind an idiot , fool, liar from any direction.

★ Yours tribe attracts your tribe.

★ Everything happens for a reason, crazy and proud of it.

★ I hope karma will slap you in face before i do.

★ Why life keep teaching me lessons i have no desire to learn sometimes.

★ If plan "A" doesn't work the dictionary of alphabets has 25 more letters stay cool.

★ No intelligent species would destroy their planet.
★ Love vs like pluck a flower or water it daily.

★ The who understand it understand life buddha.

★ Once you believe signs are every where.
★ You cant force a connection we meet the right people at the right time under right circumstances through natural vibration.

★ A man is complete until he has married then he is completely finished.

★ Don't be afraid to change. You may lose something good but you may gain something better.

★ One mistake and very one judges you.

★ It is better to be hated for what you are than to be loved for what you are not learn from everyone and follow no one.

★ A wise man fills his brain before emptying his mouth.

★ Recognise the divine power within be your own guiding light elevate yourself with consistent efforts practice and self discipline 2G.

★ Be someone light when they are hopeless.

★ People laugh because I am different i laugh because they are all the same.

★ People tell i have a bad attitude just because i speak what they keep thinking.
★ Be the hero of your own life story.

★ For all those men who think a woman's place is in the kitchen remember that where the knives are kept.

★ But with the presence of mind.

…….. Thank You ……
Saurabh Bhatnagar

Printed by Books on Demand GmbH, Norderstedt / Germany